The Hover Kids
1 Sky Pirates

Story by Cameron Macintosh

Illustrations by Alex Lopez

The Hover Kids 1: Sky Pirates

Text: Cameron Macintosh
Publishers: Tania Mazzeo and Eliza Webb
Series consultant: Amanda Sutera
 Hands on Heads Consulting
Editor: Sarah Layton
Project editor: Annabel Smith
Designer: Jess Kelly
Project designer: Danielle Maccarone
Illustrations: Alex Lopez
Production controller: Renee Tome

NovaStar

Text © 2024 Cengage Learning Australia Pty Limited
Illustrations © 2024 Cengage Learning Australia Pty Limited

ISBN 978 0 17 033387 0

Cengage Learning Australia
Level 5, 80 Dorcas Street
Southbank VIC 3006 Australia
Phone: 1300 790 853
Email: aust.nelsonprimary@cengage.com

For learning solutions, visit **cengage.com.au**

Printed in China by 1010 Printing International Ltd
1 2 3 4 5 6 7 28 27 26 25 24

*Nelson acknowledges the Traditional Owners and Custodians
of the lands of all First Nations Peoples. We pay respect
to Elders past and present, and extend that respect to
all First Nations Peoples today.*

Contents

Chapter 1   Stolen Clocks   5

Chapter 2   A Perfect Plan?   8

Chapter 3   The Tower Trap   15

Chapter 4   Clocks and a Pot   22

The Hover Kids

Ari

Cait

Jed

Chapter 1

Stolen Clocks

It was Tuesday morning. Jed, Ari and Cait were heading to class.

"Did you hear the news?" Ari said to the others. "Another big clock has been stolen from an old clock tower!"

"Another one?" asked Jed. "Where did the thieves strike this time?"

"The town hall tower on Rumble Road," replied Ari.

"That was the last big clock in the city!" said Cait. "It must have been the sky pirates again."

"What do you think the pirates are doing with all the old clocks they've been taking?" asked Ari.

"I don't know," said Cait, "but there's a reward for anyone who can help the police catch the thieves!"

"Do you mean ... money?" asked Ari.

Cait nodded.

"Are you both thinking what I'm thinking?" asked Ari.

"Yes!" said Jed. "Maybe with the reward money, we'd have enough to get booster jets for our hover scooters!"

"We need a plan," said Cait. "Let's meet in the library at lunchtime."

Chapter 2

A Perfect Plan?

All morning, Jed, Ari and Cait found it
hard to pay attention in class.
They were trying to think of a plan
to catch the sky pirates. At lunchtime,
they met in the library.

"I have an idea," said Ari. "Let's make a
pretend clock and put it in the Rumble
Road clock tower. The sky pirates will
wonder why there's a new clock, and
they'll come back for it."

"We can set a trap for when they come!"
said Jed.

"Great idea!" cried Cait. "Let's make the
clock tonight."

That night, Jed, Ari and Cait rode their
hover scooters to Jed's gran's house.
Using some cardboard and paint from
Gran's garage, they made a clock face that
was just the right size for the clock tower
on Rumble Road.

They hovered on their scooters to the top of the clock tower and put the pretend clock face in the empty space.

"It looks perfect!" said Jed.

"Well, kind of perfect," said Cait, laughing.

The next morning, the new clock face was big news!

Breaking News: Clock Suddenly Reappears on Rumble Road

"Now we just need to set our trap," said Jed. "And I know just what we can use!"

Later that night, Jed, Ari and Cait hovered back to the top of the clock tower with a large net. They parked their scooters beside the flagpole on top of the tower, and waited.

After a few hours, the pirates still hadn't appeared.

"I want to go to sleep," said Jed.

"Me too," said Cait.

"Just five more minutes!" said Ari.
"Don't forget that reward!"

Chapter 3

The Tower Trap

Just as Ari was ready to go home, too,
a ship floated up to the clock tower.
It looked very old and had lots of holes
in its sides.

Jed, Ari and Cait looked over the edge of the tower, down at the ship. Just as one of the pirates leaned over to grab the clock, the three children got on their scooters and dropped the net down. The net fell onto the ship's mast. The ship tipped onto its side as the pirates flew around the flagpole, trying to break free of the net.

Just then, Cait pressed a
button on her scooter.
"I've sent a message
to the police!"
she called out.

The pirate ship pulled hard, spraying out steam behind it. As the pirates tried to pull away, the flagpole bent further and further towards the ground.

"Oh, no!" said Jed. "It's going to break!"

As the flagpole made a loud groaning noise, they all heard the sound of police sirens.

As soon as the police were close enough, they tied the pirate ship to one of their jets, cut the net and towed the ship back towards the station.

"Well done, young detectives!" said Captain Chang, the police chief. "We've been trying to catch these pirates for years! Come and see me tomorrow."

Chapter 4

Clocks and a Pot

The next morning, Captain Chang took Jed, Cait and Ari to a garage nearby. Inside, they saw many stolen clocks and a huge pot.

"The pirates wanted to melt the clocks down in this pot," said Captain Chang. "They were going to use the metal to make parts to fix their old ship."

"Now," she said, "here's your reward for catching the pirates!"

"Thanks!" said Jed. "This will help us get booster jets for our hover scooters!"

"We can hover across the skies and look out for anyone else getting up to mischief!" said Cait.

"I'd like that very much!" replied Captain Chang.

A week later, all the stolen clocks were back in their towers, shining in the sunlight.

"Well done, clock detectives!" said Ari to Jed and Cait. "The Hover Kids are the best, hands down!"